WIN FROM WITHIN

Finding Yourself by Facing Yourself

STUDY GUIDE

Also by John W. Gray, III:
I Am Number 8: Overlooked and Undervalued,
but Not Forgotten By God

WIN FROM WITHIN

Finding Yourself by Facing Yourself

STUDY GUIDE

John W. Gray III

Faith Words

New York Nashville

FaithWords
Hachette Book Group
1290 Avenue of the Americas, New York, NY 10104
faithwords.com
twitter.com/faithwords

First Edition: October 2018

ISBN: 978-1-5460-3587-9 (trade paperback)
Printed in the United States of America

LSC-C
10 9 8 7 6 5 4 3 2 1

Table of Contents

A WORD FROM THE AUTHOR

We live in a culture that is obsessed with being #1. Particularly in America where we think we are #1 in nearly everything. We aren't winning though. On any level. We only think we are because our metrics for success are the number of cars we have, the sizes of our homes, our positions on our jobs, and how many likes or followers we have on social media.

None of that means anything in God's economy.

What I've come to learn is that God's idea of victorious living is the opposite of what we have been taught about the American Dream. Victory is the laying down of your will and mine in favor of God's will. It's a laying down of our personal preferences in favor of God's perfect plan. The devil is looking for every opportunity to shoot his shot in your life. He wants to decimate you. He wants to divide you. He wants to break you and minimize your influence. He tried this very thing with Jesus during our Lord's forty days of fasting in the wilderness. But what the devil didn't know was Jesus had a spiritual reservoir that superseded even physical hunger.

And maybe to the untrained eye, as Jesus hung on that old, rugged cross, it looked like He'd lost and satan had won. But no, oh no, Jesus didn't lose a thing. He won it all! Our redemption was His prize, Praise God! And when He stepped out of that tomb on the third day, He redefined what winning looked like. For us, He redefined forever what victory will be.

Victory looks like resurrection. Part of us must die, so the authentic, God-designed part may live.

So much of the tension in our lives is because of the distance between our projected images and our actual selves. Ultimately, we must get to the point where, like Jacob, we are so tired of running from who we are that we fall deep into the grace-filled arms of our Savior. That's where our peace is found. And ultimately that's where we will win at life. Success is found in uncovering our true identity in Christ and developing deep, abiding relationships that support our full godly actualization and our purpose in Him. I hope this study guide will offer you success in finding your true self.

Each chapter corresponds with the chapters in *Win from Within* and, through stories, questions, and activities, will allow you to drill down to the marrow of your own heart.

I wrote *Win From Within* because I wanted to use my own story—my own life—to stir you up and shake you into realizing that you are absolutely worthy of being the best you possible. You are worthy of winning. Forget that surface desire to show up people at your twenty-year class reunion. Be a winner because that's what God created you to be. Just be willing to win God's way. This path isn't easy but, I assure you, winning from within is 100 percent worth it.

John W. Gray III

Chapter One

Mama's Boy

"The earliest definition of who we are usually comes from the people who influenced us."

When we grow up in families and environments that cannot fathom the calling on our lives, it's terribly easy to feel insecure and unworthy. We might even find ourselves putting the God-ordained desires of our hearts on the proverbial shelf in order to appeal to those with shallow expectations for us. As a result, we experience this ongoing battle between who we, deep down, know God created us to be and our history and generational leanings. But despite it all, we must decide to believe God. We must understand that the word God has spoken over us will never ever return void. It doesn't matter how long it takes for us to come to ourselves, how many times we sabotage the journey to our destiny, God is there, waiting to nurture the gifts He's placed in us.

Jacob understood that all too well in our text for this chapter. And so does our first fictional friend on this journey, Julia.

MEET JULIA

My mother never thought I'd be anything. I don't know why. Every time she got a chance, she would take a dream that I had and smash it into tiny pieces. For instance, I remember at eleven years old wanting to be a dancer. I'd watch graceful female dancers on television and become completely enthralled as they moved across the stage. Watching them made me so happy, and I felt my heart fill up with joy every time I saw a dancer. It didn't matter if the dancer was a ballerina, in a musical on Broadway, or a jazz performer. When I witnessed Michael Jackson moonwalking for the first time on live television, I knew deep down there was something in me that was drawn to dance. I began to practice in my room. I would extend my legs out across the bed and lean over, stretching as though I was a ballerina on a bar.

One day, my mother observed one of my impromptu ballerina sessions. She seemed to have been standing there in the doorway for a good while watching. When I finally noticed her, I turned, smiled, and said, "Mommy, I think I want to be a dancer when I grow up." I thought she would finally encourage me. But I should've known that was never her way.

She looked at me and smiled. Her voice was eerily calm. "You'll never be a dancer. I don't see it. You don't have the skills, and I don't have the money to waste on lessons for you to get the training even talented dancers need to make it."

All I heard is "I don't see it," which my eleven-year-old mind translated to "I don't see you." It hurt me to my core, so much so that over the next few years, I began to act out. I found ways to get in trouble in school, at church, and anywhere else I went. I was never the same after that moment.

I ended up going to college, but majored in journalism, only because my best friend was a journalism major and talked about how cool it would be for us to start our own magazine. After graduation, I worked for a few publications and quickly figured out that being a writer wasn't for me, so I took a customer service job with the phone company and have been working there ever since. I will probably retire from there in a few years.

Six months ago, my mother passed away. Before she died, I had an opportunity to sit with her in the hospital. One evening, a few days before she transitioned, she turned to look at me, her eyes filled with tears. I thought it was the pain of her illness, so I asked her if she wanted me to call the nurse. She shook her head. Her words were simple, yet moving.

"I am so sorry."

"Sorry for what, Mama?"

"I am so sorry for holding you back."

I didn't get it at first. It had been more than twenty-five years since that day she stood in the doorway and told me what I would never be. I thought I'd forgiven her for the things she said to me as a child that had so negatively affected me. Until she apologized, I didn't even realize how much of that devastation I had carried with me all those years.

"I didn't know how to help you," she went on. "I didn't know how to encourage you. I didn't know how to push you toward your dreams. No one ever pushed me toward mine, and I just didn't know how."

In that moment, I realized that so much of my experience of my mother was related to what she had experienced herself. She only knew what she knew. It was a revelation. It also hurt, and it left me stuck for a long while because I was now long past the age when one becomes a dancer.

A few days later, I came across a flyer that announced adult dance classes beginning at a local community center. *Maybe I won't dance for the American Ballet Theatre or on Broadway*, I thought, *but it's never too late to be who I was made to be*. I tentatively signed up. Since the first class, I haven't looked back. I'm asked to dance in staged programs in my community, I lead the dance ministry at church, and I mentor girls who dream of becoming dancers in schools in the area.

REFLECTIONS ON JULIA'S STORY

Very much like Jacob and the prophecy that was given to Isaac about him becoming heir to his family's estate (see Genesis 25:21-27), Julia had a specific gift and calling on her life. But instead of stealing the gift like Jacob did at the encouragement of his mother, Julia, also at the encouragement of her mother, chose to forgo her gift.

Write about a time when you were young when you knew God had called you to do or be something, but you gave it up because of a lack of support from those closest to you.

___

___

___

___

___

___

___

___

___

In what specific ways can you return to and honor that calling today and going forward?

WORK IT OUT

Fill in the missing words of this popular scripture verse from Colossians 3 (ESV):

"Children, __________your parents in __________ , for this pleases the ____________."

Fill in the missing words of this popular scripture verse from Exodus 20 (ESV):

"__________ your __________ and your ____________ , that your ____________ may be long in the land that the Lord your _________is giving ___________."

Fill in the missing but most telling of Rebekah's words from Genesis 27 (ESV):

"His mother said to him, 'Let your _____________ be on me, my son; only ________ my ___________, and go, bring them to me.'"

List ways you might reconcile these passages. Consider what it means to obey and honor a parent or family member who might be telling you to do something (or not do something) that doesn't align with God's will.

FOR GROUP DISCUSSION

In order to ascribe a value to yourself that wasn't sown into your life by your parents or those who had early influence on you, how have you operated in your own strength, without God?

POSTWORTHY:

Using the hashtag #winningGodsway, pose the following question on one of your social media accounts and make note of the discussion that follows:

Is there a way to obey and honor your parents AND follow the will and callings of God when those two things are in conflict?

Recall times when you have manufactured a persona or manipulated situations in order to fill the void of not doing what God was calling you to do.

How have you seen this play out in your life? What has been the impact of operating this way?

With your group, discuss ways each person can hold another accountable to not continue these patterns of thinking and behavior.

EMPOWERED TO WIN—GOD'S WAY!

There is an ongoing battle between our flesh and spirit; our history and our calling; our nature and the prophetic word God spoke over our lives at the dawn of time. To overcome this and truly win in our lives, we must continue to pray and seek God's face in order to stay in alignment with His perfect will for our life.

But seek first the kingdom of God and his righteousness, and all these things will be added to you. – Matthew 6:33 (ESV)

MY DAILY PRAYER

Open my eyes, Father, to the ways in which my past has informed my present. Teach me to forgive and to move forward with the dreams You gave me long ago. Help me to, no matter what, stay in alignment with Your will for my life. In Jesus' name, amen.

MY WIN FROM WITHIN TAKEAWAYS ARE:

Chapter Two

Where Is Your Altar?

"Prioritize the presence of God over the cares of life."

There is a moment when everything changes for us. Sometimes it happens early, in our twenties, as we navigate "adulting" and all that means. For others, it happens later in life when we've done all we can do in our own strength and are now exhausted enough to turn to the One who can truly redirect our lives. Either way, those moments of decision are critical and impact us for a lifetime. This is why it is important to prioritize the presence of God in our lives. When we are faced with life-changing decisions, we can take a moment to rest, recharge, and then respond according to what we know God is saying to us, pushing away our fleshly desires. It's especially important that once we get the answers we are looking for, even when they don't look like what we'd anticipated or hoped for, we can praise and worship God because we trust that He knows what's best for us. Ask Sharon.

MEET SHARON

I'm not proud of the *way* I made it to the top of my career. I had all the right degrees and worked hard to be a corporate executive for a multi-billion dollar company. But along the way, I've had to step on a few people to get to where I am. I readily admit it. It's the nature of the beast and the M.O. of this environment. The work I do also requires me to make sacrifices and, unfortunately, some of that sacrifice has taken my time and attention from my family and my friends. Worst of all, I've had to sacrifice my personal character.

I remember a young woman who asked me to mentor her. She saw me as someone she could identify with, grow alongside, and learn the ropes from. At first, our relationship was exactly what she needed. I shared with her what I knew and taught her how to navigate the treacherous world of business. But then, she got good—*really good*. Too good.

My boss was the CEO and suggested to me that my mentee come to work in my department. I knew what that meant. I'd hit the glass ceiling at the company. She was younger and more skilled. I was faced with a decision. I could continue to develop her and believe that God would protect my own position or give me something better, or I could ensure that she never rise to my level. Deep down in my heart, I wanted to do the former. I did! But the pressure of the job, the realization that I'd never make more money than I was making in that moment and couldn't afford to lose it, caused me to make a different choice.

She trusted me, and I set her up for a fall. She ended up in trouble over a minor issue that I'd orchestrated behind the scenes. She was demoted and transferred to a different department. She didn't know of my involvement and reached out to me, asking for help to figure out what happened. I never responded. She ultimately ended up leaving the company.

What I did was so terrible, but I felt cornered and didn't feel like I had a choice. But I did. I had a choice.

One day, I came into my office and looked around at the plaques and awards. I felt sick; I literally wanted to vomit. Everything about what I had acquired—the corner office, the parking space, the perks, the travel—none of it mattered. I laid my head on my desk, and for the first time in a long time, I prayed. I asked God for help. I repented and asked God to help me become better. I told God that something big had to happen because I could not continue to live outside my character anymore.

That prayer was interrupted by the knock on my door that changed my life. My assistant said my boss wanted to see me. When I entered his office, I felt a clarity and peace in my heart I wouldn't be able to explain until much later.

He let me go that day, ironically, for a reason I still can't determine. I wouldn't be surprised if someone who was trying to retain his or her role at my expense orchestrated it. Funny how reaping works, huh? When I returned to my office to pack my things up, I got on my knees and praised God like I was at the church altar. I didn't care who heard me. I also laughed harder and more fully than I'd laughed in a while. I smiled, I cried, and I praised God because, in a strange way, I knew I would be all right. For the first time in a long time since climbing the success ladder, I knew God was there. He was with me.

REFLECTIONS ON SHARON'S STORY

In Genesis 28, Jacob comes to a "certain place" where he finally lies down to sleep. This place seems to symbolize a point of no return for him. For us, it's the point where everything changes, and we can't go back to the way we were. Why do you think Sharon's "certain place" occurred when it did? Consider the moments in your own life when you were faced with a decision to change course.

What are some of the turning points in your own life—those moments when God turned your life upside down in order to reveal His purpose and plan for your life—and what was your response in those moments?

WORK IT OUT

God knows where you are. He knows what He placed inside of you. He may have even given you a glimpse of what's to come early on in your life. But sometimes we are blinded by our circumstances and our past. Jacob had done so much dirt. He was on the run, and now he was tired. Think about the sequence of events in the scripture passages below (Gen. 28:10-22 ESV) in light of your own personal circumstances. Below this table, write what the Holy Spirit is saying to you through the Word.

Jacob left Beersheba and went toward Haran. [11] And he came to a certain place and stayed there that night, because the sun had set. Taking one of the stones of the place, he put it under his head and lay down in that place to sleep.	Weary from running, Jacob finally gives in to his exhaustion and rests.
[12] And he dreamed, and behold, there was a ladder set up on the earth, and the top of it reached to heaven. And behold, the angels of God were ascending and descending on it! [13] And behold, the Lord stood above it and said, "I am the Lord, the God of Abraham your father and the God of Isaac. The land on which you lie I will give to you and to your offspring. [14] Your offspring shall be like the dust of the earth, and you	While sleeping, in a vision, God reveals Himself to Jacob and confirms the call on his life.

shall spread abroad to the west and to the east and to the north and to the south, and in you and your offspring shall all the families of the earth be blessed. [15] Behold, I am with you and will keep you wherever you go, and will bring you back to this land. For I will not leave you until I have done what I have promised you." [16] Then Jacob awoke from his sleep and said, "Surely the Lord is in this place, and I did not know it."	Jacob awakens and realizes that nothing can ever be the same again. His life is forever changed.
[17] And he was afraid and said, "How awesome is this place! This is none other than the house of God, and this is the gate of heaven." [18] So early in the morning Jacob took the stone that he had put under his head and set it up for a pillar and poured oil on the top of it.	Jacob worships God at the place where the change happens.
[19] He called the name of that place Bethel, but the name of the city was Luz at the first. [20] Then Jacob made a vow, saying, "If God will be with me and will keep me in this way that I go, and will give me bread to eat and clothing to wear,[21] so that I come again to my father's house in peace, then the Lord shall be my God, [22] and	Jacob moves forward with peace and a mission to live right before God and humanity.

this stone, which I have set up for a pillar, shall be God's house. And of all that you give me I will give a full tenth to you."	

FOR GROUP DISCUSSION

Sharon's decision to worship God when she got fired is a perfect demonstration of winning looking a whole lot like losing from the outside. Why is it good to praise and "build an altar" to God as a response to His redirection?

POST-WORTHY:

You haven't been called by God, if you haven't first been broken by God. #winningGodsway

As a group, identify other scriptures and biblical accounts that reveal praise and worship as the appropriate response to these turning points.

EMPOWERED TO WIN—GOD'S WAY!

Jacob's reaction to God's vision to him was to, right in the moment, build an altar to praise and worship and acknowledge what God had done. Jacob, like Sharon, had the veil removed from his eyes and recognized that God had been with him all along. God's grace is sufficient for us (see 2 Cor. 12:9). He gives us time to get things right. But when we come to our stopping point and can identify that God is present, that's when we grow spiritually. That's when we truly win!

MY DAILY PRAYER

God, help me to always take a moment to praise You for the work You are doing in my life. Even now, I lift my heart to You in worship for I know that You are here and walking this journey with me. In Jesus' name, amen.

MY WIN FROM WITHIN TAKEAWAYS ARE:

Chapter Three

Birthright Gone Wrong

"Temporary hunger is not worth sacrificing an eternal promise."

Imagine I came to you with a proposition. I wanted to make a trade. Having grown up in New York City, where public transportation is the primary mode of getting around, you'd waited until well after college to get your driver's license. Having finally done that, you were excited about driving for the first time. I told you I wanted to give you a brand new Mercedes Benz. Your mind is blown! You've always wanted a Benz. Not just for status reasons, but also because you'd heard that they are great cars that last a long time. There's a catch, though. In order for me to give you the Benz, you have to give me your house.

At first, you are taken aback. This is your home. You've lived there forever. You own it free and clear with no mortgage or debt because your grandmother left it to you in her will. You might think you would never do something so obviously wrong. You would never choose a depreciating asset, like a car, over real estate—something that will have more value in the long run.

But then you think, *Well, I didn't exactly pay for the house*, and *When will I ever make enough money to buy a Benz? This is a once-in-a-lifetime thing.*

You start to rationalize: *I could live in an apartment for a while. I could probably get more attention if I pulled up to work in a Benz.*

You're probably screaming at this page now, thinking *NO! Don't do it!* Hmm, let's review that again: You are sure that you would never trade something of greater value for something that meets a temporary but deeply felt desire? It happens more often than we care to admit. And not just with Esau and other biblical figures. Let's see what Damon has to say.

MEET DAMON

I'd just gotten a scholarship to one of the best schools in the country—a full ride! My entire family was so excited. My mom couldn't help but rave about me to her friends at work. My dad would point at me from across the sanctuary at church, and I knew he was talking up my accomplishment. I was the first one in the family to go away to college and...I was scared out of my mind. I'd worked so hard to get to this point. I'd gotten a 4.0 grade point average and was the valedictorian of my class. I'd done so well and worked so hard at pleasing everyone. But I was tired—I didn't know how much longer I could sustain the whole "good kid" thing. Don't get me wrong, I loved school. I liked learning and was looking forward to going to college. But I'd also begun to feel like there was a level of perfection required of me that I no longer aspired to. I was so tired of what I thought were unreasonable expectations that I was willing to do anything—and I mean anything—to break free from them. Even for one night. And I did.

On graduation night, some friends and I decided to go to a party and then grab some food at a local diner afterward. It was so much fun. We laughed and talked about our old teachers. Everyone talked about the colleges they were going off to and how they were all looking forward to be free of the "rules" when they got there. I didn't talk much about my school. Everyone was so excited that I didn't want to spoil the fun.

One of my friends who was not going away to college, but was entering the military in a couple of weeks, suggested that we do something crazy. Our last hurrah, as he put it. He said that he and his cousin in another state used to "dine and dash"—that's where you eat food and then run off without paying for it. Most of the group was down with it, but I was nervous. I'd never done anything like that before. I ran through the outcomes in my mind. Best-case scenario would be that we wouldn't get caught. We'd head home and no one would know what we did. Worst-case scenario would be that we'd get caught, the restaurant would press charges, and I'd spend the night in jail for stealing. It was a risk, for sure. But as I said, I was tired. I needed something to break the monotony of being the good dude. So I agreed and we concocted a plan.

Once our waiter was distracted, one of us went to the restroom. We wanted everything to look normal. The waiter came by and asked if we needed anything else, and one of my friends asked for a glass of water. As the waiter turned to get the glass of water, the person that was in the restroom came out and left out the door. We ran out behind him.

When we got outside, we took off running in the parking lot and dived into the car. The driver, my pre-military friend, pulled out fast from the parking lot. The tires screamed as he sped down the street. That's when we saw the lights. We were being pulled over by the police. We all sat terrified and quiet in the car as two police officer walked over on either side. I don't think I've ever been more frightened in my entire life. The officers asked for us to step outside of the car, and we put our hands up and did exactly that.

One officer asked us where we were coming from. Before we could answer, the other officer got a call saying that some kids had skipped paying at a restaurant. We were busted.

But it got worse. At the party earlier, I'd decided to try smoking weed for the first time. My friend gave me a joint, but we couldn't find a lighter. So I put it in my pocket thinking I'd maybe give it try later. The police officers began patting us down, and as they were checking my pockets, guess what they found?

When the cop pulled the joint out, my heart sank. Everything changed. I knew it had, even before he put the handcuffs on me. I'd given up an amazing opportunity, sacrificed it, for a moment of revelry and rebellion that I would never be able to take back. When the arrest was reported to the high profile civic organization that gave me the bulk of the monies for my scholarship, it was rescinded. I could no longer afford to attend the college of my dreams and ended up at a local, state school. My parents' disappointment was palpable, but even worse was how I'd let myself down.

REFLECTIONS ON DAMON'S STORY

Like Esau, Damon made a decision in the midst of his own weariness that was far from wise. He traded something that would have long-term value (going to a great college) for something that would only satisfy his longings in the moment (having wild fun with friends). List some specific ways Damon could have dealt with his feelings without sabotaging his future.

When you reflect on your own life, can you identify moments when you gave up something of greater value for a temporary pleasure? Write about why you think you made that choice and, in hindsight, what you would have done differently to preserve your "birthright"?

WORK IT OUT

Review the chapter once more. In it, I talk about four ways we can prevent ourselves from making bad decisions in the midst of our physical, emotional, or psychological exhaustion. Hint: When you don't do these four things, the result is that you are "constantly running, constantly doing, and constantly working." I've provided you the first letter of each action. Fill in the remainder of the word and then next to it list three ways this action can show up in your own life.

R________________

1.
2.
3.

R________________

1.
2.
3.

R________________

1.
2.
3.

A________________

1.
2.
3.

FOR GROUP DISCUSSION

Galatians 6:9 says, "And let us not be weary in well doing: for in due season we shall reap, if we faint not" (KJV). At the top of a sheet of paper (or in a new social media post), write, "I am tired, Lord. Help me!" Then have everyone in the group write or post words, phrases, or scripture verses that offer practical but godly ways to deal with our weariness. Discuss how these words, phrases, or verses can help a person not *trade their house for a Benz*.

EMPOWERED TO WIN—GOD'S WAY!

Many times we end up trading our long-term benefits for short-term pleasure, not because we are dumb, but because we don't understand the value of what we have. But even in those moments, it's important to push past our fleshly desires and hold fast to the promise that our "latter will be greater" (see Job 8:7). Even if we don't understand our call, or we are tired of the uphill climb to reaching our purpose and destiny, we must keep our faith in the One who called us.

POST-WORTHY:

Whatever we are looking for outside of God will never fully satisfy us. Too often we run in the direction of our need and not to the God who supplies all our needs. #winningGodsway

MY DAILY PRAYER

Heavenly Father, give me clarity of vision so that I don't sacrifice my purpose for short-term pleasures. Help me to believe that even in moments when I can't see my blessing I can trust You are working all things out for my good.
In Jesus' name, amen.

MY WIN FROM WITHIN TAKEAWAYS ARE:

Chapter Four

Blind Ambition

"Work from validation and not for it."

Jesus' words in the Garden of Gethsemane are powerful and revealing: "My Father, if it be possible, let this cup pass from me; nevertheless, not as I will, but as you will" (see Matt. 26:39).

How different would the story of our Lord and Savior Jesus Christ read if we saw Him wielding His power as the Son of God to make things happen for the Father? What if, instead of humbling Himself by picking up a cross and carrying it to Golgotha, He turned the cross into a weapon and took out His enemies like a first-century Marvel superhero? It might make for a fascinating read, but it would not be what God intended. Jesus relinquished His power as He walked the earth and chose to solely serve the purposes of God. His motives were pure, and He never acted out of self-preservation. He had the most power but the least ambition because He understood that everything He did was not for the validation and approval of people, not for His own elevation, but for the glory of God and the fulfillment of God's will in His life. It took a devastating blow to the heart for our friend Troy to learn not to use his gifts and callings for his own selfish ambition.

MEET TROY

There was absolutely a succession plan in place. I was the man who was supposed to replace my father as pastor of the church I had grown up in. It was an inheritance of sorts. I had done everything my father asked of me, everything I knew to do to get the position, even when there was something else on my heart.

I'd felt called to the mission field ever since I took a trip to New Orleans after Hurricane Katrina. I had a different perspective on missionary work. So many of my friends from the Christian college I attended for undergrad talked about going to Africa or Asia to do their work, but I felt that there were so many people I could serve right here in the major U.S. cities. It baffled me that people would be willing to go serve halfway around the world but resisted traveling two miles into to a different part of their own hometown. I would have loved to continue working and serving in this way, but I felt obligated to uphold the mantle of my father. And, honestly, I loved the access following in my father's footsteps would afford me. His popularity as a pastor would certainly lead to my own. At least that's what I believed.

After a long sabbatical, my father called me one day and told me to meet him at his office to talk about the pastorate. I remember being so excited to finally begin to see what the next step would be. That space in my soul that yearned for something else seemed filled by my desire to establish myself in the city as a "powerful voice" as one national news outlet referred to my father. I had finished four years of seminary, and gotten my master's degree in counseling. I'd preached my first sermon over a decade prior and had taught Bible studies for the last seven years. So when I walked into my dad's office, I was sure that he was going to outline what the transition would look like. And I suppose that's what he intended to do also.

Before I sat in the restored antique chair that was positioned in front of his huge desk, I stared at him and—maybe for the first time—saw the age that hung from the lines near the corners of his eyes. His face revealed both the wisdom and compassion that our congregation held in such high esteem. They looked to him for guidance and direction because he was the consummate shepherd: available, accessible, and challenging. I sat down just as he began slowly to speak.

"Son, as you know I'm going to be retiring soon."

"Yes, Dad."

"And upon my retirement, the board will be looking for my recommendation for a replacement pastor."

I nodded.

"I have recommended that you serve as an interim pastor until the board decides on who will take the official position."

I was confused. Interim pastor? Maybe he was saying that I needed to be interim pastor until the board decided to select me as his successor. His eyes pierced me.

"Son, I am also recommending that you are not considered for the official pastor position."

I was stunned.

"What do you mean, Dad? I mean, this is what we've…I mean…I've been working toward."

"You absolutely have. It would have been my absolute joy to have you succeed me in this role."

I shook my head. "So what's the problem? You know the board will listen to you."

"The problem is, it's not up to me or the board. God makes the call and, after much prayer—wrestling, really—I've surrendered to His will in the matter."

"Dad!"

He put his hand up. "Son, you've put in a lot of effort. You've done the networking with key members of the congregation. You've been doing everything you can to work toward becoming the pastor of this church…" He paused for more than a beat, then continued. "…even though *being* a pastor of this church is not God's call on your life."

I went silent.

"I've been around a long time, Son. Too long, some would say." He chuckled. "And I discern that the reasons why you want to take this position has nothing to do with what God has called you to, and everything to do with pleasing me and lifting yourself up. That's not what I want for you."

I was still silent. The emotions were bubbling just under the surface. I was desperately holding my tongue.

"Son, I know it's hard to hear, but you will not succeed me as pastor."

I was angry. And sad. I had so many questions. If he knew this, why didn't he tell me before? Before I did all of this work. But I knew the answer to that. I'd set myself up for this very thing. I'd forgotten Who was sovereign and had the final say. Now *that's* who was redirecting me on my path.

REFLECTIONS ON TROY'S STORY

How does ambition show up in Troy's story?

What was missing from Troy's efforts to become pastor of his father's church?

Think of a time when you worked incredibly hard to make something happen for yourself (in business, school, or relationships) only to find out that God had a different and better plan for you. What did God reveal to you about yourself by undoing your personal ambition? How was the outcome ultimately better than what you had in mind?

WORK IT OUT

It's important to be able to identify selfish ambition so that when it comes up in our own hearts, we can recognize it and lay it on the altar. Read the scripture passages below and, in the box next to it, write how selfish ambition shows up for the person(s) in the passage.

Scripture	Notes
Cain (Genesis 4)	
James and John (Matthew 20)	

Absalom (2 Samuel 13-18)	

FOR GROUP DISCUSSION

Pair up with someone or work in groups of no more than three individuals. Discuss the following questions:

- In what specific ways have you submitted your personal ambitions to God, and what did that process reveal about you?
- In what areas of your life are your ambitions currently not submitted? Why do you think you are resisting it?
- What is one thing you can do on a daily basis that would help you release your selfish ambitions to God?
- What checks and balances will you put in place to help you continue to live without selfish ambition?

After your discussion of where each member of the group stands, pray the following prayer together:

Lord God, thank You for revealing to us the areas where we have run ahead of Your will for our lives. We want to continue to pursue our purposes in You, but we know that we must operate within Your will and timing. Strengthen us as we submit to You those tasks and opportunities that we know are out of alignment with what You have for us. Show us the moves You want us to make solely for You. We desperately desire to serve You, O God, and to not advance any personal agendas because we know that in Your Kingdom the last shall be first and the first, last. Help us to be more like Jesus, understanding the power of the Holy Spirit that lies within us, but not wielding it like a weapon. Abba, please guide us as we hold each other accountable on this journey toward complete surrender and the unearthing of our authentic design in the process. In Jesus' name, amen.

POST-WORTHY:

What we call ambition is a response to the things that are absent in our lives. Submit your ambition to God to get an accurate picture of who you really are. #winningGodsway

EMPOWERED TO WIN—GOD'S WAY!

In an effort to figure out our purpose—why we're born—we can easily find selfish ambition rising up in us. That kind of ambition causes us to be unnecessarily competitive, seeking validation from people instead of trusting that God has already made us enough. We might even end up doing things that aren't in alignment with God's intended identity for us. Selfish ambition is costly when it goes unsubmitted to God. Allow God to use your ambition to reveal who you are and then turn it into a mechanism for godly service.

MY DAILY PRAYER

Jesus, help me to never be so consumed with my success and elevation that I end up missing You or hurting others. Lead me to ways I can remove personal ambition as a driver for my service on this earth. Thank You for showing me the areas in my life that need healing in this regard. In Your name, amen.

MY WIN FROM WITHIN TAKEAWAYS ARE:

Chapter Five

Running for Your Life

"Return to the place you are running from; the wounding place."

Running feels natural when we believe something big and scary and dangerous is chasing us. We run from danger, both real and perceived. Viewing our pasts as big and scary enough to run from gives it power that it should not have. If we truly believed God redeems us and that repentance is the way to deliverance, we wouldn't run away from our past; we'd run toward it. We'd run back to the places that hurt us because we know that not only pain lives there, but so does our healing.

I'm reminded of some advice I was given by a friend who loves to go camping. I'm definitely not the go-sleep-in-the-woods-with-the-lions-and-tigers-and-bears-oh-my! type, but I found fascinating his answer to this question: What would you do if a bear invaded your camp site? Apparently, my answer (run as hard and as fast as you can) is not correct (but likely what I'd do anyway). The correct answers: #1, be still; #2, use a calm voice; and #3, never run but move slowly, cautiously, always keeping your eyes on the bear. The first action allows you to assess the situation and the second allows the bear to identify you as human. The third allows you to move appropriately in the right direction.

This is an incredible blueprint for how we might approach our past.

#1 Be still. Pray and ask God what you need to know about *your* return to your past.

#2 Stay calm. Remind yourself that you are a different person returning to your past. I'm Israel, not Jacob, Sir!

#3 Don't run. Running doesn't prevent your encounter with the past, but it does reveal your fear, making you more susceptible to being overpowered by it. Look at the wound for what it is, for what it taught you, and for how God has or is currently using it for your deliverance. Lynn hasn't quite gotten there yet, but her journey is just beginning.

MEET LYNN

I was a teenage mother, and although I loved my daughter dearly, I carried so much guilt and shame because of that pregnancy. That shame caused me to act out against my parents and other authority figures in my life. I knew I had disappointed them, but I struggled with finding my way back to myself, back to who I knew they had raised me to be.

My anger, which had gone unchecked even since before I had gotten pregnant, was full blown and out of control. I constantly ranted about feeling like everyone was against me or judging me. One day things went too far. In the middle of a heated argument with my mom, I threw a lamp across the room, narrowly missing my mother and scratching, though only lightly, my toddler. I'll never forget the look on my mother's face as she held my baby girl in her arms. I was sure my mother would never forgive me, so I packed up my bags and moved two states away with the family of some friends.

Although I would phone to speak to my daughter, I stayed away for nearly three years. It was entirely too heavy a load for me, thinking about what I'd done. I'd hurt the people I loved the most in the world. Over time, it became more difficult for me to get up the nerve to return. I'd told my mother "I'm sorry" over and over again for years, but the look on her face still haunts me. It was like she didn't recognize me. I was a different person, someone she could not have birthed. If her face had a sound, it would have crashed like a heart breaking in two.

Guilt and shame were tiny seeds that had taken root in me and later flourished. It kept me away from my family. It kept me away from my daughter. I knew I needed to go back. I needed to find the courage to do it.

REFLECTIONS ON LYNN'S STORY

Like Jacob once he realized his brother sought to kill him for stealing the birthright, Lynn ran from the consequences of her actions. How might she have better dealt with the guilt and shame she felt for disappointing her family members? Write an alternative ending to her story that demonstrates an outcome shaped by perseverance and not running.

Think about the ways you have sought relief from the pain of your past in wrong ways. Did running relieve you of the consequences of your past? Rewrite those scenarios so that you don't run but embrace the truth of what happened or what you did. What feelings come up for you when you consider facing your pain?

Evaluate those feelings against the truth of what God says about you (see Phil. 4:13, Ps. 46:5, 1 Cor. 15:10, Rom. 5:8, 1 Pet 2:9, Ps. 139:14). Now list the potential outcomes of not running and how different those are from what is currently happening.

WORK IT OUT

Part of facing your past is telling the truth about what exists there. God wants us to not only submit our ambitions to Him, as noted in the previous chapter, but He also wants us to submit our pains and past to Him. Which of the following do you find most challenging to face and release to God?

- A lie you told about someone
- A lie about you that became truth in the eyes of some
- A sin you committed against someone
- A sin committed against you
- A choice you made that you know didn't align with God's will
- A relationship you were involved in that wasn't God's best for you
- Some other pain:

  ____

Write at least one way you can reconcile the pain in your past and surrender it to God for good. For example, you might call "that person" and ask them to meet you for coffee. You might write a letter to your deceased family member and read it to them at their gravesite or in a special or sacred place.

____

____

____

____

____

____

____

____

FOR GROUP DISCUSSION

To stop running can be challenging if you've spent most of your life doing exactly that. It's a vulnerable place to be, and sometimes we need help. We need someone we trust to walk alongside us. If you feel safe, share your plan for reconciliation with the group. If it's a person you need to face, have one person in the group sit in a chair and pretend to be that person as you share your heart with them. If it's a situation or circumstance you must return to, ask someone in the group to go with you or to be available to you as you make the journey back to that wounded place.

POST-WORTHY:

God is committed to developing us. He desires for us to reflect His glory. Facing our pain, the things we run from, is part of His sanctification process. #winningGodsway

EMPOWERED TO WIN—GOD'S WAY!

Our healing often lies in returning to the place where we were wounded or where we did some wounding. With courage and integrity, we tell the truth about our lives. We do this not to wade or wallow in our pain. It is not a form of self-abuse. The goal is to face what happened, repent, get clarity, and move forward on our journey to destiny.

God is not just committed to our winning; He's committed to our development. In fact, winning and growing are intricately connected. Every single thing that has happened to us has a purpose—yes, all of it—but we can never arrive at that purpose if we keep running away. It's time to let the Author and Finisher of our faith rewrite our narratives. He wants to turn the life you've orchestrated back into the life He originally had in mind for you.

MY DAILY PRAYER

Abba, I surrender my story to You. Transform how I see winning and success. Give me the strength to embrace this new mind. Develop and shape me into the person You had in mind as You formed me in my mother's womb. In Jesus' name, amen.

MY WIN FROM WITHIN TAKEAWAYS ARE:

Chapter Six

Hi, My Name Is...

"The power of God can change the narrative associated with who we've been."

I've said it over and over, and I will scream it from the rooftops if I have to: God can change your story. He will shift you and transform you into a better version of yourself, the version He had in mind all along. But one of the biggest challenges we face when our lives begin to change is the encounter we have with people who knew us "way back when." It's human nature to be drawn to brokenness. Think about all the times you clicked that link, excited about the "tea" you would get about someone's life. Too often, we are drawn to people whose brokenness makes us feel better about our own. But in truth, we don't have to allow those negative perceptions of us to penetrate our hearts. The only thing we are called to do is make sure that the new life God has given us aligns with who Jesus has called us to be. It's not easy to shake the voice of those who used to know us. Jonathan knows that better than anyone.

MEET JONATHAN

I had a colorful life in my early twenties. Okay, so that is probably just a nicer way to say a life filled with drug addiction and crime. I was introduced to meth at 16, and by the time I was 22, I was a full-blown addict. After being kicked out of my home, I began robbing people to support my habit. When I was 23, I got caught robbing a woman at an ATM and was arrested.

During my trial, the judge said something that changed my life. He said that if I continue on the path I was on, I would be dead within a year. "Either the drugs will kill you, or you are going to rob the wrong person," he said. He explained that he could see this was not who I was. There was more to me than this addiction that had run my entire adult life thus far. Instead of sentencing me to jail time, I ended up spending an extensive amount of time in an intense drug rehabilitation program.

After I completed the program and my five years of probation ended, I stayed clean. I went to college and ended up moving away from my hometown for a job. In my new city, I am a different person. People view me as this successful businessman, married to a smart and beautiful woman, with two lovely children. We go to church every Sunday and Bible study every Wednesday. I volunteer at the local Boys and Girls Club in hopes of intervening in some young man's life the way the judge intervened in mine.

Everything sounds great, right? A classic redemption story. It is, except when I return home. Each time I return to my hometown, I'm confronted with the comments and the stares. The judge was right. Most people expected me to be dead, so when I show up healthy, sober, and with a modicum of success, they are shocked and surprised. All that would be fine if shock was the extent of it. But even members of my own family like to periodically throw in my face the time I stole their television or the time I got caught robbing a neighbor. I can't seem to escape my past when I come home, and I feel like I relive it every single time I'm there.

REFLECTIONS ON JONATHAN'S STORY

One of the reasons many of us don't stop running from our past is because we are afraid that people will never be able to look beyond who we once were. But the truth is the evidence of God in our lives is way more powerful than an individual's or group's perception of us. This is how our tests become our testimonies. List three ways that Jonathan might deal with his family and friends. (Do not include <u>not</u> going back home.)

Write a dialogue that Jonathan could have with his family and friends when they bring up his past.

Family: "You're doing so great now. It's hard to believe you stole our television when you were doing drugs."

Jonathan:

Family: "Remember that time you got caught robbing Mrs. Smith next door? She still locks her door when she hears you're coming home. Hahaha…"

Jonathan:

Consider a change you've made in your life. How have the people around you responded to that change? How do their responses make you feel? How do you manage those feelings so that they do not consume you or make you slide back into old behaviors?

WORK IT OUT

Complete this self-assessment to affirm the changes God has made in your life and to think about what changes need to happen in the future.

Who am I?
Am I okay with what I've learned about myself? Why or why not?

Is the person I described who I want to be?

Is the lifestyle I described what I want to be known for?

FOR GROUP DISCUSSION

Play the "They say, I say, but what does God say?" game!

Each person in the group should fill out the first two columns of the following table on their own. The objective is to identify what people might say about us based on who we were in the past. It's also an opportunity to tell the truth about what we think about ourselves in this pivotal moment of transition and change. Each person in the group should share what they've written down and, as a collective, the group will help each individual align or counter the outside and self-narratives with what God has said about him or her. Use Scripture as the basis for what "God says!"

"They say" I am...	"I say" I am...	"God says" I am...

EMPOWERED TO WIN—GOD'S WAY!

When we are willing to face the truth of who we've been, God will not only rewrite our story, He will extract value from the negative parts of our past. Because our old nature is covered in the blood of Jesus, God redefines us. God gave Jacob a new name. God gives us a new nature—the character of Christ. Every day we must be vigilant in making sure that our character lines up with this new nature. This is ultimately how we grow spiritually and how we will win in everyday life.

MY DAILY PRAYER

Father, sometimes, if I'm honest, I'm scared. It's hard to face my past. But I trust You completely, and I know that I'm covered by the blood of Jesus on this journey. Thank You for the new character You are developing in me. Thank You for the courage to stand firmly in my new truth even as I face old ones. In Jesus' name, amen.

POST-WORTHY:

We have to be honest about our true condition and surround ourselves with people who will tell us the absolute truth. #winningGodsway

MY WIN FROM WITHIN TAKEAWAYS ARE:

Chapter Seven

Dreams and Ladders

"God is never caught off guard by any situation that occurs in our lives."

In my experience, when someone talks about having a spiritual encounter, too often people respond with what images on television and film have taught them. They think of seeing dead people and heads turning 360 degrees on folks' necks. The truth is God is engaging with us supernaturally every day. The Holy Spirit is active in helping us get out of our own way and realize the potential that has always resided within us. Whether that's moving on an employer's heart to give a job to someone who may not look the best on paper but who they sense could add value to the company, or giving someone a vision for creating a product or service that will revolutionize how humans exist (those of you who read on a Kindle or iPhone would agree, right?), the Spirit of God is working on our behalf. He is totally not surprised by anything that has happened or will happen in our lives. In fact, God desires for us to eliminate any preconceived notions about where we come from and what we have access to, and simply asks us to press toward the mark (see Phil. 3:14-15). Just like Charlene, when He adds His super to our natural, great things can happen.

MEET CHARLENE

"I'm not supposed to be here," I kept saying to myself. "Says who?" was the response that reverberated in my spirit. I'd just been offered a position as the director of a nonprofit organization. I was finally going to be able to serve people in all the ways I'd felt led to over the years. But much of my life up to that point would have never pointed to this outcome.

I was molested as a child and later placed into foster care. I aged out of the system and, at eighteen, found myself homeless. One day, while looking for food, I made my way to a local church's soup kitchen. It just so happened that the first lady of the church was serving the meals that day. I remember how she looked at me as I sat there devouring the pasta and bread. She sat down next to me and just stared. I have to admit that I felt very uncomfortable at first. I didn't have much. I wasn't dirty or anything, but I certainly didn't look like someone she with her beautiful crown of braids and soft eyes should be taking the time to look at. But she kept me in her gentle gaze and then asked what seemed to be odd questions: "What do you want to be? What do you want to do?"

"At this point," I said, "a cashier at Burger King would be nice."

"Dream bigger," she said.

Her words shook me. "I don't know. Manager then?"

She laughed so loud and heartily that I thought her stomach would burst.

But that was the start of something. I would come there every day to get food, and she would ask me what I wanted to do and tell me to dream bigger. She later invited me to her home—not to visit, but to stay until I received my GED and could get into the local community college.

And now, it's eleven years later, and I am here, the director of a nonprofit organization, serving individuals with mental health challenges. I am so grateful. I don't know how this came to be, but I'm so grateful that it did.

REFLECTIONS ON CHARLENE'S STORY

Like Charlene, there are many of us whose stories would indicate a different outcome in our lives. We are living testimonies to God's faithfulness. Think of three areas of your life where God has shown up in ways you could never have imagined.

Take a moment to write a prayer of gratitude for all the ways God has turned your life around. Consider every area from family relationships to career paths to ministry/service opportunities.

WORK IT OUT

Create your own dream ladder. Mark the rungs at the bottom of the ladder with all the things that you might do to pursue the will of God in your life. (Example: Spend more time in worship. Register for school. Find a prayer partner. Write a grant.)

Next, prayerfully consider how the Holy Spirit might move on your behalf—these are things that are not within your control—and mark those on the rungs at the top of the ladder. (Example: Open a job opportunity. Heal back pain.)

FOR GROUP DISCUSSION

It's incredibly important that we quiet the spirit of unbelief as we move toward winning God's way. The sovereign and magnificent nature of God means that He is able to do things in our lives that will completely and utterly blow our minds. Think about Jacob. God literally showed him in a dream that, yes, you've been a rotten scoundrel, but I'm going to give you a house. No, wait. That isn't it. What did God promise Jacob? Oh, that's right! "Your descendants will be like the dust of the earth, and you will spread out to the west and to the east, to the north and to the south" (see Genesis 28). Talk about mind-blowing!

In your group, have your own dream session! Write on a dry erase board or a new post the following question:

"What is the most mind-blowing thing God could do in your life right now?"

Then, every member of the group should search their imaginations for that very thing and write it on the board. Afterward, discuss how it felt to take the limits off God. Remind each other that what's on the board/post doesn't even begin to

POST-WORTHY:

Whether it is in our dreams, in the silence, or in other unexpected ways, God is always speaking. #winningGodsway

touch what God is capable of doing in our lives. He is most certainly the God of "exceedingly, abundantly" (see Eph. 3:20).

EMPOWERED TO WIN—GOD'S WAY!

Jacob's dream reveals God's desire to work in partnership with us. The ladder was symbolic of the partnership between heaven and earth, the practical and the supernatural. Yes, if we rely on solely the practical—what we can see or hear—then there will be many things that should disqualify us from serving God. But with God's supernatural involvement—His ability to resurrect dead things—we can be healed and can move forward toward purpose. God will certainly call us, but we must move on the call. We must do our part.

MY DAILY PRAYER

Jehovah, You are the only One who has the ability to supernaturally change my life, and I'm so grateful to partner with You in that work. Thank You for resurrecting those parts of me that needed to be healed. I'm so grateful for Your deliverance. In Jesus' name, amen.

MY WIN FROM WITHIN TAKEAWAYS ARE:

Chapter Eight

Pot, Meet Kettle

"Sometimes the hardest person to see is ourselves."

Have you ever noticed that the person you like the least often has the most in common with you? It's usually someone who you don't "care for," but you "can't put your finger on" why. In fact, one of the worst feelings in the world is the moment when you realize that the person you've been hating on forever is actually someone who—surprise!—struggles in the exact same area as you do.

God uses people to show us who we are. He uses people as mirrors to reflect back to us our true character. It's not because He wants to humiliate us or make us feel bad about ourselves. It's because He wants to admonish us to stay the course and continue to grow in Him. Michael's recent encounter was proof of this very thing.

MEET MICHAEL

We've been in counseling for close to a year. It's interesting being a pastor in marriage counseling. I'm so used to being on the other side of the room. I'm used to being the one who's giving the advice, the suggestions, the exercises, and the role playing. Now I was sitting next to my wife on the couch, opening my heart about an affair I'd had two years prior. It was the most heart-wrenching thing to do, but if I was going to save my marriage, it was necessary.

Counseling has been good for us. We've been able to work through the issues and traumas that we both brought into the relationship. I've been able to admit that there was more than just lust factoring into my behavior—there was a hole in my soul I was trying to fill, and instead of asking God to fill me, I sought "help" in the bed of another woman. It's funny how you can be in the midst of redemption, working on yourself, growing and changing, and just when you think things are turning around, you end up faced with the very thing that you spent so much time trying to escape.

I was sitting at lunch with another pastor friend of mine. We were chatting about our congregations and the often mundane things that happen as one is serving in ministry. Suddenly, his phone rang, and he looked at the screen and said, "I'm sorry, I need to take this."

What followed was a conversation that was strangely intimate for it to not be his wife. I knew it wasn't her because he'd just told me that she'd gone to a spa with some friends and would not be picking up the phone for a few hours. The way he was speaking to the woman on the phone left no doubt in my mind that this was a mistress. And when he hung up, he confirmed it.

"Yeah, you know how it is." He winked.

I wanted to judge him, but I couldn't. I *was* him only a couple of years removed. But I was also angry. I was angry because here I was sharing my heart with someone I thought was a mentor to me only to find out that he was struggling with the same issue. That's when I knew that this journey was going to reveal way more about me than I'd initially thought.

REFLECTIONS ON MICHAEL'S STORY

When confronted with his mentor's infidelity, Michael was reminded of his own failures. How can he use his reminder as a way to fortify the work he is doing in counseling? How might he respond appropriately to his mentor in that moment?

List some ways to manage the inevitable emotional response that comes with encountering someone who reflects the negative aspects of your own character.

WORK IT OUT

Make a short list of all the significant individuals in your life. It might look something like this:

Wife/Husband
Daughter
Parents
Boss
Best Friend

Next to each name, list the traits about them that you like the least. That list might look something like this:

Wife/Husband – Control freak
Daughter – Strong willed
Boss – Micromanager

Now prayerfully consider how these traits trigger some knowledge about yourself that you are struggling to face. Is your spouse's controlling nature triggering feelings of inadequacy? Do you find that you micromanage your children in the same ways that your boss micromanages you?

FOR GROUP DISCUSSION

Read the following passage with your group (or post online) and discuss some practical ways to live out these verses:

> *Brothers, if anyone is caught in any transgression, you who are spiritual should restore him in a spirit of gentleness. Keep watch on yourself, lest you too be tempted. Bear one another's burdens, and so fulfill the law of Christ. For if anyone thinks he is something, when he is nothing, he deceives himself. But let each one test his own work, and then his reason to boast will be in himself alone and not in his neighbor. For each will have to bear his own load. – Galatians 6:1-5 (ESV)*

POST-WORTHY:

Be careful. That negative person in our lives might just be a reflection of the negative attributes in ourselves. #winningGodsway

MY DAILY PRAYER

Thank You, Father, for the people You have placed in my life by design. [List each individual on your list from above] *Every day I learn so much about my own character as a result of my interaction with them. Lord, please help me to see myself more clearly so that I don't project my own struggles on people who are only walking their own path toward deliverance and healing. Jesus, I plead the blood over my mind, heart, and soul. Keep me ever awakened to Your pruning as I press toward becoming worthy of Your call. In Jesus' name, amen.*

EMPOWERED TO WIN—GOD'S WAY!

The principle of reaping and sowing is very real (see Gal. 6:7). We must be conscious of the words and deeds we are sowing into the earth so that we are not surprised by our harvest. And sometimes God will show us who we are, the areas of improvement we need to make, and even the consequences of our future actions by bringing someone into our lives who serves as a mirror. Part of the sometimes-painful process of self-discovery is allowing God to reveal our true character through the people around us.

MY WIN FROM WITHIN TAKEAWAYS ARE:

Chapter Nine

Face-to-Face

"The time-lapse between your past and your confrontation actually demonstrates the presence of God's grace."

We can learn a lot about ourselves by simply assessing the value we place on the people and things in our lives. Some say owning a home is more valuable than renting an apartment. That's the American Dream, right? Others believe that if one has to work twelve hours a day, six days a week in order to own a home, it's not worth the time lost with family and friends. They place more value on cultivating relationships than the acquisition of property. Neither of these perspectives is inherently wrong. So what does God say?

Rather simply, *none* of it matters to God.

As humans who, by nature, create hierarchies and categories in order to make sense of the world around us, we tend to wrestle with what we believe is or is not valuable. And yet God is very clear that the only thing that is truly valuable is His presence in our lives. It's only the presence of

God that gives anything we have value. Jobs, positions, money, or status—whether within or outside of the church—become false gods when pursued without God's approval. And, as Bonita learned, God will only extend His grace for so long before He decides to unravel our busy, carefully curated, yet empty lives.

MEET BONITA

I knew something had to change but couldn't figure out how to get there. My life had become nothing but constant movement. I was the one who would proudly proclaim, "Oh, I'll rest when I'm dead." Boy, I didn't realize how close I came to exactly that. I spent every waking hour somewhere other than at home. I worked eight hours a day as an executive assistant. I served in my church as a deacon, a Sunday school teacher, and women's group leader. I was the president of the PTA at my children's school. And, not to sound proud, but I was so good at all of it. Okay, so maybe there is a little pride there. I just believed in being excellent, no matter what. I'd had a rough childhood, having fought my way out of poverty and despair. So I believed that I had to work hard all day and all night at whatever I did. It's what I did in order to maintain my sense of self.

But then it happened.

Everything fell apart.

The church split because of an indiscretion of the senior pastor. Out of nothing but a need for familiarity, I chose to stay with the pastor and the church I'd worked so hard in. But because of the reduction in the congregation, I lost my position as a Sunday school teacher and women's group leader. Later that same month, my job laid me off, and I lost the election for my second term as PTA president. I literally had nothing at that point.

Well, scratch that, I did have something. Something I'd stopped paying attention to for a good while; I had my family.

God in His grace and mercy didn't allow me my prophecy of "resting when I die" to come to pass. I had my health.

But who was I if I couldn't actually *do* things? I didn't know, and that was the problem. I thought I could work my way into some kind of acceptance. But God had been waiting. He let me run that race for a while. But when the time came for me to grow, God shut everything down to show me what was most important.

REFLECTIONS ON BONITA'S STORY

So much of the busyness we see in today's culture is masked by this notion that productivity is necessary at all costs. God, however, says "everything in season" (see Ecclesiastes 3). There is a time to sow and a time to reap. There is also a time for Sabbath rest. What are some of the risks we take when we choose to remain in a perpetual state of busyness and distraction?

God is certainly not saying we shouldn't work or serve or even work and serve. In Proverbs 6:6-11, He actually calls out the lazy person, encouraging a kind of systematic way of working. But when our working becomes a way to avoid sitting still and hearing the voice of God, then God will allow a situation to occur that will force stillness upon us. In what ways might you have ignored God's call to slow down or pace yourself? Pray about ways you can find moments throughout the day to tune yourself in to the Holy Spirit's voice and direction.

WORK IT OUT

As noted earlier, slowing down often means being forced to hear the voice of God and deal with the false personas we've crafted. God wants the authentic you, not the projected you. Use the chart below to make a list of characteristics that might be the projected you. These are parts of your personality that don't feel right, but you keep around because they fuel a perception that gains acceptance.

An example: The projected you might be the "never let them see you cry or sweat" person you've become at work. Your coworkers might use words like "strong" and "rock" to describe your personality. However, the authentic you might actually be sensitive and empathetic. Because you view empathy as a weakness though, you bury that part of yourself and craft the image of the "rock." Meanwhile, you are dying inside because, in truth, you are not hard. You were built for emotional expression and vulnerability.

Projected You	Authentic You

FOR GROUP DISCUSSION

Read the following passage from Luke 10:38-42 (MSG) as a group.

> *As they continued their travel, Jesus entered a village. A woman by the name of Martha welcomed him and made him feel quite at home. She had a sister, Mary, who sat before the Master, hanging on every word he said. But Martha was pulled away by all she had to do in the kitchen. Later, she stepped in, interrupting them. "Master, don't you care that my sister has abandoned the kitchen to me? Tell her to lend me a hand."*
>
> *The Master said, "Martha, dear Martha, you're fussing far too much and getting yourself worked up over nothing. One thing only is essential, and Mary has chosen it—it's the main course, and won't be taken from her."*

Next, assign three individuals the roles of Mary, Martha, and Jesus. As a role-playing exercise, act out these verses for the group. Once the short skit is finished, have an open discussion where each member of the group shares the characters they most identify with and why.

POST-WORTHY:

God is willing to bring us to a point of complete submission by setting us apart from everything we hold dear. He will quiet the noise and make stillness our only option. #winningGodsway

EMPOWERED TO WIN—GOD'S WAY!

God will let you run yourself ragged—for a season. He'll allow you to continue to manufacture a persona that is as far away from your authentic self as the east is from the west—for a season. God is so incredibly gracious in that way. But then we must come face-to-face with the monuments we've built and be willing to lose it all. That's what #winningGodsway means: giving it all up so that God can unlock His blessings for you.

MY DAILY PRAYER

Dear God, I've come to the end of myself. Thank You for showing me who You created me to be. Help me shed the "me" I've manufactured and worn as a mask. I truly desire to be free, and I know that freedom is only found in You. Thank You for Your love. In Jesus' name, amen.

MY WIN FROM WITHIN TAKEAWAYS ARE:

Chapter Ten

When the Past Comes Knocking

"God factored in your humanity when He called you."

Here is something I hope is as much a relief to you as it was for me: God is not surprised by anything you've done. He's not surprised by anything you are doing. He will not be surprised by anything you will do in the future. The beauty of His omniscience is that He knows everything. And yet, every day, in light of what He knows, God calls men and women to do great things for Him. This is why running and hiding from a past mistake—whether it's Jacob from Esau or our friend below, Calvin—is futile. We cannot escape God's challenge. We cannot escape God's love. And here's the blessing: it's the latter that drives the former.

MEET CALVIN

It was only a matter of time before someone caught on. I don't know if I was necessarily hiding him as much as I just didn't want people to know about that part of my life, about the mistakes that I've made. Not that my child, my son, was a mistake. Maybe the sexual activity was, but not the child. Nevertheless, no one besides my mother and one cousin who I talked to often knew about the child I'd had out of wedlock. Honestly? I had an image to protect. People saw me as someone to look up to. I'd been leading the youth Bible study at church for a couple of years now, and so many of the teenagers there saw me as a model for what it meant to be a good Christian man. How could I tell them that I'd fallen off? How could I tell them that I'd made a mistake and the consequence was that I was a baby daddy?

But I knew I wasn't going to be able to keep the secret for long. The mother of my child wanted a relationship that I wasn't willing or ready to give. She was becoming more vocal about my involvement in my son's life. The last thing I wanted was my child to feel rejected or abandoned because I wanted to keep up appearances. I was stuck though. I wasn't sure if being transparent with the youth group or my pastor was a good idea, or if it would just end up with me categorized as another fallen leader. I didn't want that on my resume, nor did I want that attached to my character. Even if it was true.

REFLECTIONS ON CALVIN'S STORY

Regret is powerful. Too many of us are holding on to regret so tightly that we have become stagnant, unable to move forward with our lives. Calvin was so hung up on what people might think about him that he forgot that the way we truly overcome is by our testimony (see Rev. 12:11). If you were faced with Calvin's challenge, how would you go about introducing your role as a parent to those you are accountable to (the pastor and youth)?

Some of Calvin's resistance to sharing his son with the church was rooted in not wanting to admit that, yes, he had fallen. Consider how you handle your mistakes. Is your inclination to seek reconciliation, hide it, or deny it altogether? Spend some time journaling the reasons for your approach.

WORK IT OUT

We often condemn ourselves in areas where God has already forgiven us. Romans 8:1 says, "There is therefore no condemnation to them which are in Christ Jesus, who walk not after the flesh but after the spirit" (KJV). Take the following steps toward shifting the way you think about the sins of your past:

1. Ask God to reveal to you the areas of your life where you have hidden or denied your mistakes/sins out of fear of discomfort or lack of acceptance. Name them specifically and examine your reasonings for such a response.

2. Commit to releasing those mistakes once and for all, allowing the blood of Jesus to do its perfect cleansing work. Outline specific ways you will counter the voices (internal and external) that will inevitably rise up to condemn you all over again.

3. Revisit ways God has already shown His grace toward you. Make a list of blessings that have come or ways God has used you, despite what you may or may not have done in the past.

FOR GROUP DISCUSSION

Write a new script! As a group, come up with a twenty-second script that everyone can say to themselves or aloud whenever they feel condemnation weighing them down. Anchor the script with Bible verses that affirm how much God loves us, in spite of us.

EMPOWERED TO WIN—GOD'S WAY!

You've stopped running. You've given it all up. And now you are standing naked before God, feeling vulnerable and unworthy of what He wants to give you. God is truly relentless in His love for you. Like Jacob, He will wrestle with you deep into the midnight hour. You aren't disqualified simply because you made bad decisions. The enemy wants to keep you mired in who you were, and God wants you to see yourself through His eyes. Your victory is rooted in your ability to do exactly that.

POST-WORTHY:

Whether publicly or privately, exposure is coming because God doesn't let any of us get away. He loves us entirely too much. #winningGodsway

MY DAILY PRAYER

Thank You, Jesus! I praise and honor You. Your love has sought me out and healed my heart. I will no longer search for my worth in people or things. I am now whole in You. Continue to show me who I am and where You are leading me. I want to see myself through Your eyes. In Jesus' name, amen.

MY WIN FROM WITHIN TAKEAWAYS ARE:

Chapter Eleven

Allow Me to Reintroduce Myself

"When God puts His hand on you, you're never the same."

Perseverance will always birth greatness. The ability to endure long after we have exhausted our abilities is a special kind of surrender that I believe God truly honors. (Remember Jacob's wrestling match?) Particularly in our relationships, if we are willing to face our truth and push through the condemnation that will try to settle into our hearts, God will not only change how we see ourselves but ultimately how we are seen by others. Reconciliation is imminent, as our friend Lynn from chapter five learned.

MEET LYNN...AGAIN

I thought they were going to hate me. The day I decided to come home, my anxiety was through the roof. My therapist had prescribed me some medication to help me get through the day, but even that had begun to wear off. I had to face the truth: I abandoned my only child more than three and half years ago. The only thing she'd known of me were phone calls and video messages. I felt like I had thrown everything away, so how could there be anything left when I returned? But I had to find out. I was tired of running. I had to find out if there was any love left for me there. Even if there wasn't, going back was the right thing to do.

When I knocked on the door and my mom opened it, I was overwhelmed with what happened next. She pulled me into her so close I could smell the scent of her perfume. She loved *Chloe*—always kept a full bottle on her dresser. I used to get into it when I was little and douse myself until my eyes stung. Her embrace reminded me of that sweet memory. My dad stood off to the side, but I could see the tears in his eyes.

"Welcome home, Baby Girl," he said.

I didn't know what to make of it. I thought that everything I had done made it so that I could never be forgiven. It sounds ridiculous now, but I truly thought that they would never love me as their daughter again. What I later came to find out was that their love had never changed, I did.

My parents parted like the Red Sea and standing behind them was the most beautiful little kindergartner one could ever see. Her pigtails were wrapped in little balls like Princess Leia in *Star Wars*, and she smiled widely at me. "Mama."

One word. That's all it took. I ran over and picked her up in my arms. I kissed her forehead, and her nose, and her cheeks, and her chin. The love had never gone anywhere. God's grace was truly sufficient for me.

REFLECTIONS ON LYNN'S STORY

The single thing we all need in order to push forward into a new identity is courage. Lynn returned home despite being afraid of what her parents would say or think. As Henry Cloud once said, "The pain of remaining the same had become greater than the pain of change" for her. Examine and journal about the ways you might reconcile unhealed relationships or circumstances despite the presence of fear and doubt.

WORK IT OUT

In this chapter, I provided a three-M method for identifying and addressing where you are in the process of winning God's way. Fill out the table below by writing words, names, and phrases that represent the corresponding models, mirrors, and moments that have been revealed to you through prayer and this study.

MODELS: The forces that shaped you. Your history and family dynamic.	
MIRRORS: The people, places, and things that help you become aware of who you are and who you can become. They reflect your true self back to you.	
MOMENTS: The defining point in time when you are ready to move forward in your new identity. It's Jacob leaving his wrestling match with the name Israel. It's the open door to greater.	

FOR GROUP DISCUSSION

Discuss the following questions in a small group or online:

- What does it mean to you to "die dry"?
- Why are we sometimes unwilling to share our ideas and dreams with each other?
- Have there been pivotal moments you have clearly missed because you were afraid? Is it possible to reclaim those moments and, if so, how?

EMPOWERED TO WIN—GOD'S WAY!

God wants to change your name—not your actual name, but who and what you are called. He wants to reintroduce you to world as the whole and healed person you've become. Your former identity is no longer valid. And soon, those whose vision of you has been narrow and misinformed will have no choice but to see the touch of God on your life. They will have no doubt that you've changed and will, like Esau, welcome you with open arms. The moment has come for you to walk in the fullness of your new self.

POST-WORTHY:

The grace and power of God is truly found in Him redefining, repurposing, and restoring us to our authentic selves. #winningGodsway

MY DAILY PRAYER

Father God, I'm so grateful that You have repositioned and re-introduced me. Guide my responses as I encounter those who may not yet understand or accept the changes that have taken place in my life. I receive Your counsel and look forward to standing firm as Your disciple. In Jesus' name, amen.

MY WIN FROM WITHIN TAKEAWAYS ARE:

Chapter Twelve

Winner Leaves All

"To win, we must lose our wills to the will of the Father."

The late soul singer Sam Cooke's most popular song is the heart-wrenching ballad "A Change Is Gonna Come." What I love about the lyrics is that the thread pulled through every verse is hope. Despite the pain, despite what the singer's circumstances might look like, despite what the world says he can or cannot do, he is adamant that change is just around the corner. That is a proclamation of faith.

But once change comes, where does it go? What do we do with it? I would submit that all the transformations God allows us to experience are purposed to break the generational curses in our family lines and to leave a legacy for the children that will come after us—our own children and the children God sends us during the course of our lives. As the elders often say, there will be no U-Hauls following the hearse at our funeral. We can't take anything with us. Tiffany knows that better than most.

MEET TIFFANY

"You have to finish the will," my attorney said.

I know that death is imminent. I no longer feel the need to beat around the bush and mince words anymore. Even if it isn't this horrible cancer that's commandeered my body, I am going to die one day, and when I do, I want to leave all that I've accumulated in this life to my children and their children.

My babies come to visit me every day, and I'm grateful for that. I've been in the hospital this go-around for about two weeks, so I know that this isn't the case for everyone here. Tony brings me macaroni and cheese. I probably shouldn't be eating that, but at this stage he wants to make me happy. And of course, it's his special macaroni and cheese! He doesn't know that the restaurant he is thinking about opening will be a resounding success, and he will have all he needs to make it so.

My daughter Allison comes to visit me every other day, and on the weekends when she doesn't have to work. She loves to braid my hair, and the feel of her hands on my scalp is like heaven already. She doesn't know that she's a healer, but I do. Her touch has the power to bring people back from the dead, even if it's just an emotional or mental resurrection. Whatever she attempts to do will be successful because of the gift of her healing touch.

And then there's my baby boy, Mason. He just comes and sits with me. Doesn't say much. I know he's hurting and dealing with a lot seeing me here in this state. He's often stoic or writing in that little brown notebook he carries everywhere. He thinks I'm asleep, but I see him as he fiercely marks those pages with his thoughts. He doesn't know yet how great he will be. The stories he will tell will be stories that people will share for hundreds of years—long after both he and I are gone.

I suppose I should get about the business of writing this will. There are the details of money and property, yes. But there's something more I want to leave to my children—I want to leave them a legacy of kindness. I want them to know that their gifts will make room from them, but it will be the character and integrity that hopefully I've been able to instill in them that will keep them wherever they go.

REFLECTIONS ON TIFFANY'S STORY

When one is faced with mortality, there is generally a clarity that comes. Tiffany made peace with her diagnosis, and while she was open to God healing her, she was fine if that healing occurred on the other side of this life. Because she was clear, she had a chance to speak life into her children. When you consider your own mortality, what thoughts come up for you? What do you want to be known for after you have transitioned?

____

____

____

____

____

____

____

____

____

____

____

WORK IT OUT

Leaving a legacy is not just about leaving money and things. It's not just about leaving behind a financial inheritance. God calls us to leave everything on the table. He desires for us to leave a legacy that reveals the fruit of the Spirit in our lives. Our names should not just be synonymous with "billionaire" or "celebrity." We should want our names to be synonymous with "joy-filler" and "peace-maker." Make a list of things unrelated to money you'd want to leave behind as a legacy.

FOR GROUP DISCUSSION

Write on a dry erase board (or in a post) the following:

I will leave behind a legacy of…

Each person should then share/post a word or phrase that represents the legacy you'd want to leave behind. Write the word on the board or in a comment. After completing two to three rounds, ask each individual to select a few words and look for scriptures that confirm that legacy as valid.

POST-WORTHY:

We must declare a powerful and positive destiny, not just over the children we have birthed naturally, but all children who may be broken, vulnerable, marginalized, and bullied. #winningGodsway

EMPOWERED TO WIN—GOD'S WAY!

It's not about how much money you do or don't make. God is aware of your financial situation. It's not about the size of your platform or how much notoriety you have. God knows the degree of your influence because He gave that influence to you. To win God's way is to live a life of substance that will leave a legacy for those who come behind you. As you launch into your new destiny with your new "name," consider every action and every word as an opportunity to glorify Jesus. Steward well—and with an open hand—the positions and resources you have been given.

MY DAILY PRAYER

Lord, all that You have given me—every blessing and every lesson—has been a privilege to hold. Empower me to be a good steward of my remaining years. I pray now that You allow me to leave a legacy for future generations that will continue to make Your name great. In Jesus' name, amen.

MY WIN FROM WITHIN TAKEAWAYS ARE: